I HEAR YOU:

The surprisingly Simple Skill Behind Extraordinary Relationships

By

ADAN HASSAN

TABLE OF CONTENTS

INTRODUCTION

The most significant field for human understanding today might be relationships - how persons that are important to each other communicate. In deciding our quality of life and wellbeing, they are of prime significance. In the office, they have a major influence on productivity and efficiency. They begin wars between nations to stop them.

Based on the findings and theory founded by Dr. Murray Bowen, Exceptional Relationships teaches us how feelings effect relationships and how to function on our own portion in every partnership - the only part we can alter. The partnership continues to a higher stage through this job, where individuals report more closeness and collaboration, and a greater degree of achievement in partnerships.

First released, this significant and revolutionary book provides a clearly understandable description of Bowen's theories that have benefited thousands of people. It is a blueprint for better partnerships that explains how the concepts of the philosophy of family structures can be used in all aspects of life, including dating, families, immediate family relationships, single life, relationships with the employer, and improving one's own definition of oneself.

Chapter 1
Bowen Theory

Eight concepts

- Triangles

- Differentiation of Self

- Nuclear Family Emotional System

- Family Projection Process

- Multigenerational Transmission Process

- Emotional Cutoff

- Sibling Position

- Societal Emotional Process

Triangles

A three-person friendship arrangement is a triangle. Since a triangle is the least cohesive attachment structure, it is called the building block or "molecule" in broader emotional structures. A two-person arrangement is dysfunctional and until including a third participant, it embraces no stress. Without involving any person, a triangle may include even more conflict so the tension can change across three relationships. If the stress is too high to contain one triangle, it extends to a set of triangles "interlocking". A mechanism may relax by distributing the strain, and nobody gets resolved.

The acts of people in a triangle represent their attempts to ensure their emotional connections to significant others, their responses to too much commitment intensity, and their choosing sides in the disagreements of others. A triangle is paradoxically more secure than a dyad, but a triangle produces an odd man out, and is a very challenging place to tolerate for people. A strong force in triangles is anxiety created by anticipating being or by being the odd one out.

With increasing stress, the trends in a triangle shift. Two persons are easily near "insiders" in quiet times and the third one is an awkward "outsider." The insiders deliberately avoid the outsider, and the outsider is working to get closer to one of them. In a triangle and pressing for improvement, somebody is still uncomfortable. By preferring each other in comparison to the less attractive outside the insiders reinforce their connection. It arouses especially strong feelings of hurt whenever someone prefers another human over themselves.

The most anxious one would step closer to the outsider if mild to moderate friction grows between the insiders. The latest outsider is now one of the initial insiders, and the initial outsider is an insider.

The newest outsider is going to make predictable gestures with one of the insiders to regain closeness. Triangles typically have one side in disagreement and two harmonious sides at moderate conflict stages. The tension is not intrinsic in the partnership it occurs in but represents the triangle's overall working.

The outside role becomes the most attractive at a high degree of stress. If major disagreement erupts between the insiders, by having the new outsider competing with the other insider, one insider opts for the outside role. He wins the more secure role of watching the other two people fight if the maneuvering insider is effective. The outsider will seek to reclaim an inside role as the stress and disagreement subside.

Triangles greatly lead to the creation of psychiatric conditions. For example, a depression or maybe even a physical disorder may be caused by being pushed from an internal to an outside role, or two parents intensely stressing on what is wrong with a child may cause severe resistance in the child.

Example

During the first two years of their union, Michael and Martha were very satisfied. Michael enjoyed making big choices, and Martha was comforted by the "strength" of Michael. Martha conceived during the 3rd year of the marriage despite some trouble becoming pregnant, but it was a tough pregnancy. During the first trimester, she felt very nauseous and experienced blood pressure and extreme weight concerns as the pregnancy continued. She spoke often about her emotions over being a mother to Michael. Michael was reassuring and patient, but still started to feel dismissive of Martha for being "childlike."

Differentiation of Self

Families and other social classes have a significant influence on how people perceive, behave and conduct, but individuals differ in their sensitivity to "group thinking" and communities vary in the degree of enforcement strain they apply. This variations between persons and between groups indicate discrepancies in the levels of self-differentiation of individuals. The less established the "self" of an individual, the more influence others have on his functioning and the more he seeks to regulate others' functioning, actively or passively. The essential building blocks of a "self" are inherent, but the family interactions of an entity during childhood and adolescence decide mainly how much "self" he creates. If created unless an individual makes a systematic and long-term attempt to modify it the degree of "self" seldom shifts.

People with a badly differentiated "self" rely so strongly on others' recognition and support that either they change what they believe, speak, and do to satisfy others easily or they proclaim what the others should be more like dogmatically and push them to adapt. Bullies rely, as much as chameleons, on approval and recognition, however bullies force others to agree with them rather than agree with others. Disagreement endangers a tyrant as much as a chameleon challenges it. A severe rebel is still a badly distinguished person, but by routinely challenging others' roles, he pretends to be a "self".

An individual with a well-differentiated "self" acknowledges his realistic dependency on others, yet in the face of confrontation, critique, and dismissal, he may remain cool and level minded sufficiently to separate thought embedded in a thorough appraisal of the evidence from thinking clouded by emotionality. Thoughtfully learned beliefs help direct decision-making around critical family and societal challenges, making us less at the whim of the moment's emotions. What he is deciding and what he is doing suits what he is doing. He can behave selflessly, but his behaving in the group's best interests is a thoughtful decision, not a reaction to the demands of relationships.

Confident in his thought, without becoming a follower, he should accept the opinions of others or oppose the views of others without polarizing the disagreements. Without becoming pushy, he describes himself and struggles with demand to surrender without being wishy-washy.

Each human culture, with many gradations between such extremes, has its well-differentiated individuals, badly separated people, and people. Consequently, based on the levels of separation of its participants, the communities and other classes that make up a community vary in the strength of their interpersonal interdependence. The more severe the interdependence, the less the ability of a community to respond without a marked increase of persistent distress to potentially traumatic activities. All is vulnerable to challenges in his job and personal life, but greater susceptibility to cycles of elevated persistent anxiety for less differentiated persons and communities leads to their disproportionate share of the more severe problems of society.

Example

The instance of the triangle of Michael, Martha, Amy illustrates how in a family structure a lack of separation of self plays out in their case, a moderately differentiated unit. If Michael, Amy, and Martha were more distinct entities, the explanation that follows is about how this triangle will play out.

During first 2 years of their union, Michael and Martha were very content. He preferred to make the key choices but did not believe that he understood "the best." He still mentioned Martha what he was feeling, and he listened to her feelings carefully. Their conversations were largely thoughtful and contributed to compromises that valued all individuals' critical interests. Martha had always been drawn to the sense of duty and desire of Michael to make choices, but she still lived by the belief that she was responsible for reasoning it out by herself and asking Michael what she was thinking. She didn't presume that Michael normally understood "the best."

Nuclear Family Emotional Process

Four fundamental relationship dynamics that control where conflicts grow in a family are defined in the notion of the nuclear family emotional structure. The perceptions and expectations of people regarding partnerships play a role in the trends, but the factors that drive them mainly are part of the process framework. In intact, other nuclear family and single-parent stepparent arrangements, the patterns function.

During cycles of elevated and sustained family stress, clinical conditions or symptoms typically arise. The degree of conflict depends on the stress faced by a family, how a community adapts to stress, and the relation of a family to extended personal and family networks. The behavior of one or more of the four interaction behaviors is intensified by stress. Where symptoms evolve depends on the most active cycles. The greater the discomfort, the greater the risk that there may be serious effects and that many individuals may be symptomatic.

The four fundamental patterns of relationships are:

Marital dispute- Each partner externalizes his or her distress into the marital partnership as family stress rises and the partners become more nervous. - insists on what is wrong with the other, each seeks to monitor the other and each refuses the regulation attempts of the other.

Dysfunction of one partner: one partner urges the other to think and behave in such respects, and the other adds to the strain. To retain peace, all partners are welcoming, but one does more of it. For both persons, the relationship is relaxed up to a stage, however if family stress rises more the subordinate partner can generate so much self-control that his or her distress dramatically increases. The existence of a psychiatric, medical, or social dysfunction fuels fear, whether other required causes are present.

The partners concentrate their anxieties on one or more of their offspring. Disability of one or more children. They unnecessarily stress and typically have an idealized or pessimistic impression of him. The more parents worry on the infant, the more they rely on the child. He's more receptive to the behaviors, desires, and aspirations of parents than his siblings. The approach undercuts the separation of the infant from the family and renders him prone to acting out or internalizing family pressures. The child's anxiety can affect the output of his education, social relationships, and even his health.

Emotional distance-This development is strongly linked to the others. People separate themselves from each other to decrease the strength of the partnership, but they risk being too separated.

In some areas of the family, the fundamental partnership dynamics result in family problems come to rest. The more anxiety one entity or one partner absorbs, the fewer other entities need to absorb. This suggests that certain members of the family continue to work at the detriment of others. People don't want to harm one another but someone typically pays for it when fear chronically governs conduct.

Example

The stresses created by the relationships between Michael and Martha contribute to relational distance between them and an anxious fixation on Amy. Amy responds to the emotional over-involvement of her parents with her by creating immature expectations on them, especially on her mother.

Family Projection Process

The mechanism of family projection explains the predominant way parents pass on their relational issues to an infant. The mechanism of projecting will affect one or more children's functioning and enhance their susceptibility to psychiatric symptoms. Via relationships with their parents, children inherit all kinds of difficulties (as well as strengths), but the concerns they inherit that often impact their lives are interpersonal sensitivities such as heightened demands for affection and acceptance, trouble coping with standards, the propensity to blame oneself or others, feeling accountable for others' happiness or that others are re The infant develops greater relationship sensitivities than his parents if the prediction phase is reasonably severe. The sensitivities improve the susceptibility of an individual to effects by promoting habits that in a partnership system exacerbate recurrent anxiety.

Three phases follow the prediction process:

1. out of concern that something might be wrong with the infant, the parent insists on the child.

2. the parent interprets the actions of the infant as reinforcing the fear; and

3. The adult approaches the infant as though there is something wrong with the child.

These phases of scanning, diagnosing, and treating start and begin early in the life of the infant. The worries and expectations of parents form the growth and actions of the infant such that he learns to represent their fears and perceptions. A self-fulfilling hypothesis is one explanation why the prediction mechanism is that parents strive to "fix the issue they have diagnosed in the infant; for instance, parents consider their child to have poor self-esteem, constantly try to affirm the child, and based on their affirmation, the child's self-esteem increases.

Parents sometimes believe like they have not provided a child ample affection, care, or support, but have spent more time, resources, and consideration in this child than in his siblings. The siblings less involved in the phase of family projecting have a more mature and reality-based partnership with their parents that fosters the growth of the siblings into individuals that are less needy, less reactive, and more target-oriented. In the family projection method, all parents contribute fairly, but in differing ways. Typically, the mother is the primary caretaker and more vulnerable to undue emotional interaction with one or more of the children than the parent. Except at times of elevated conflict in the mother-child partnership, the male usually holds the outside role in the parental triangle. In relation to the infant, both parents are uncertain of themselves, but one parent typically acts confident of himself or herself and the other parent goes along. The sum of time parents invest with an infant is unrelated to the severity of the prediction process.

Example

The Michael, Amy and Martha case demonstrates the mechanism of family prediction. Before Amy was conceived, Martha's worry about Amy started. Martha was scared that she might pass the inadequacies she felt as a kid to her own child, and always felt them. This was one explanation why Martha had conflicting emotions regarding becoming a parent. Martha thought, like many others, the most essential role of a mother was to make kids feel loved. She was acutely sensitive to Amy's wishes for publicity in the name of expressing affection. Martha was there with a suggestion or strategy whenever Amy looked bored and out of sorts. She felt the path to trust and freedom for a child was in the child feeling confident in herself. Martha did not know how alert she was to some Amy indication that she may be upset or irritated and how easily she would step in to address the issue.

Martha intensely cherished Amy. In the way they were attuned to each other, she and Amy always seemed like one person. As a very tiny toddler, Amy was as responsive to the moods and wants of her mother as Martha was to the moods and wants of Amy.

Multigenerational Transmission Process

The definition of the mechanism of multigenerational transmission explains how minor variations in the differentiation rate between parents and their offspring contribute to marked differences in differentiation between the members of a multigenerational family over several generations. The data that causes these variations is conveyed across connections through centuries. The transmission takes place at many interconnected stages, varying from aware data instruction and learning to automatic and implicit emotional response and behavior programming. To shape the "self" of a person, relational and genetically transmitted knowledge interacts.

The mixture of parents consciously influencing their offspring's growth, offspring innately adapting to the moods, behaviors, and behavior of their parents, and the lengthy attachment span of human offspring results in individuals experiencing degrees of self-differentiation close to the levels of their parents. The relationship dynamics in nuclear family emotional structures, though, frequently contribute to the creation of at least one member of a sibling community a little more "self" and another member a little less "self" than the parents.

The next stage in the phase of multigenerational transmission is that people choose mates with degrees of self-differentiation that fit their own, predictably. Therefore if the "self" level of one sibling is greater and the "self" level of another sibling is smaller than the parents, the marriage of one sibling is more distinguished and the marriage of the other sibling is less differentiated than the marriage of the parents. If each sibling then has a more differentiated child and a less differentiated child than himself, one three-generational line gradually becomes more differentiated (the most distinguished child of the most distinguished sibling) and one line gradually becomes less differentiated (the least distinguished child of the least distinguished sibling). The gaps between family lines are gradually marked as these cycles recur for many centuries.

Longevity, marriage longevity, reproduction, wellbeing, educational achievements, and professional achievements can be influenced by the degree of self-differentiation. The pronounced difference that usually occurs in the lives of the families of a multigenerational family is clarified by this influence of distinction on the general functioning of life. Highly differentiated individuals have exceptionally secure nuclear families and contribute a great deal to society;

badly differentiated individuals have dysfunctional personal lives and depend heavily on others to support them. A main consequence of the multigenerational definition is that generations are deep at the origin of the most significant human challenges as well as of the highest stages of human adaptation. The multigenerational mechanism of transmission not only demonstrates the creation of "self" stages, but also shows how individuals communicate with others. The choosing of a partner is influenced by all forms of programming. For starters, if a family programmes someone to cling strongly to others and to act in a helpless and indecisive fashion, he is likely to choose a partner who not only attachments to him with similar strength, but who leads others and makes choices for them.

Example

The mechanism of multigenerational transmission helps understand the complex trends that have arisen in Michael, Martha, Amy, and Marie's nuclear family. Martha is the youngest of three daughters in an intact family in the Midwest. Martha did not feel very connected to any of her parents from her teen years on but especially to her mother. She viewed her mother as professional and compassionate, yet also negative and invasive. Martha believed her mother was powerless to satisfy her.

It seems like her sisters seemed more confident and knowledgeable than Martha. She questioned herself how she could grow up and have so many issues in a supposedly "normal household and replied that something had to be wrong with her. Her mother got interested and greatly affected Martha's preferences as she encountered significant dilemmas in her life and had decisions to make. Her mother claimed that Martha should make her own choices, but the actions of her mother did not reflect her expression. One of the greatest worries her mother had was that Martha might make the wrong choice. In time, like her mother did, Martha's sisters began to view her and viewed her as the family's infant, as one requiring special guidance. Martha's dad was sympathetic to her family's one-down role but distanced from family conflicts.

Martha despised herself for requiring others' acceptance and approval to work successfully and for believing like she did not operate more individually. She was concerned about making the wrong choice and mostly looked to her mother for assistance.

Emotional Cutoff

The definition of emotional cutoff defines individuals with parents, relatives, and other family members handling their unresolved emotional difficulties by minimizing or completely cutting off emotional interaction with them. People living away from their family and seldom returning home can minimize social interaction, or it can be minimized by people remaining in physical contact with their families while ignoring sensitive problems. If people cut off to handle them, relationships can look better" but the issues are latent and not fixed.

By breaking off, individuals minimize the stresses of family experiences, but avoid making their new partnerships too important. The more a man cuts away from his family of birth, for instance, the more he turns to his girlfriend, kids, and friends to fulfil his needs. Out of fear of jeopardizing the partnership, this leaves him prone to forcing them to be those ways for him or accommodating so much of their expectations towards him. At the beginning, new partnerships are usually smooth, however the habits that individuals attempt to avoid inevitably surface and create conflicts. By building replacement "families" with social and work relationships people who are cut off can try to stabilize their interpersonal relationships.

Everyone has a degree of unfinished connection to their initial kin, but there is far more resolution among well-differentiated individuals than among less differentiated individuals. There may take several types of an unresolved attachment. For e.g., (1) while he is alone a person acts much like a child and turns to his parents to make choices for him than he should make for himself or (2) a person feels bad when he is in more touch with his parents and feels like he needs to fix their disagreements or distresses, or (3) a person feels upset that his parents do not appear to accept or agree with him. An unfinished attachment refers to both the parents' and the adult child's immaturity, but individuals usually blame the issues on themselves or others.

People always look forward to returning home thinking this time things would be different, but typically the old relationships emerge within hours. With strong emotional undercurrents, it can take the shape of surface unity or it can deteriorate into yelling matches and hysterics. Also following a brief visit, both the person and his family can feel drained. If an adult kid holds his distance, it might be simpler for the parents. When he is in the family becomes so nervous and reactive that when he goes, they are relieved. When he is alone, the siblings of an extremely cutoff participant sometimes get angry at him and accuse him of disturbing the parents. People do not wish it to be this way, but both parties' sensitivities prohibit relaxed touch.

Example

There was no wish for either Michael or Martha to remain with their homes. Both were ready to switch east when Michael received a strong work offer on the East coast. Thanks to Michael's fantastic work offer, they told their family they were moving abroad, but they accepted the physical isolation from their families. Michael felt bad for living far away from his parents, and his parents especially Michael's mother, were upset about it. Every weekend, Michael called home and tried to mix business trips with short stays with his friends. He did not look forward to the phone calls, and during them he typically felt sad. By stressing how bad she was doing and how badly she regretted having him, he felt as though his mother had purposely taken him on "guilt trips". She never forgot to inquire whether he could be moved closer to home by his organization. Talking to his father was somewhat less depressing for Michael, but they spoke more about Michael's career and what his father was doing in retirement.

Sibling Position

The theory of Bowen integrates the study of psychologist Walter Toman as a framework for his definition of the status of a sibling. In his family study, Bowen observed the influence of sibling status on growth and actions. He considered Toman's work, though so detailed and compatible with his thoughts that he merged it into his philosophy. The simple premise is that there are unsurprisingly substantial shared traits among people who grow up in the same sibling position. For instance, older kids seem to gravitate to leadership roles, and younger kids mostly choose to be followers. The features of one position are not "better" than, nor complementary to, that of another position. e.g., with a first assistant who is a younger child, a supervisor who is an older child can operate unusually well. Younger kids may want to be in control, but usually their leadership style varies from the style of an older one.

Toman's study found that the sibling positions of partners determine the likelihood of their divorce. For e.g., if a younger sister's older brother marries an older brother's younger sister, there is less risk of divorce than if a sister's older brother marries an older sister. In the first example, the sibling or rank roles are compatible, and any partner is acquainted with residing with someone of the opposite sex. The rank roles are not complementary in the second example, though and neither partner has grown up with a member of the opposite sex. A brother's older brother and a sister's older sister are vulnerable to arguing for who is in charge; two smaller children are prone to fighting over who gets to rely on whom.

Of course, people in the same sibling position display marked variations in working. Any of the variations may be clarified by the principle of distinction. For instance, an older child who is anxiously concentrated on will grow up to be markedly indecisive and extremely reactive to demands instead of being relaxed with responsibilities and leadership. Therefore, his younger brother will become a "functional eldest," filling the family structure with a vacuum. He is the youngest child chronologically, but he develops more of the oldest child's traits than his older sibling. The youngest child who is anxiously concentrated will become an entity who is exceptionally powerless and challenging. By comparison, in a marriage, two mature youngest children will interact exceptionally efficiently and be at very low risk of divorce.

The functional features of two sibling positions are displayed by middle children. When a person has an older brother and a younger sibling, for example, she typically has some of the traits of both a brother's younger sister and a sister's older sister. It is therefore necessary to recognize the sibling responsibilities of a person's parents. An elderly child whose parents are both younger faces a distinct range of parental standards than an elderly child whose parents are both elderly.

Example

Awareness of the sibling roles of Michael and Martha and those of their parents leads to the comprehension of how things turned out in their lives. Martha was the youngest of three girls and in her household, she was the most deeply concentrated on them. In addition, Martha's mother is the eldest of four siblings and was raised in a family with a chronically invalid mother. Martha's mother was the eldest sibling, not too clearly differentiated. Her life energy was concentrated on taking care of others and leading them to the extent where she unintentionally hindered her youngest daughter's functioning. By being an indecisive, powerless, and often self-blaming girl, Martha acted out the opposite side of the dilemma. Martha's father was the youngest sibling of a five-child household.

Societal Emotional Process

In the Bowen hypothesis, each definition extends to non-family entities, such as labor and social organizations. The definition of the collective emotional mechanism explains how action at a systemic level is regulated by the emotional framework, enabling both positive and regressive cycles in a community. In how a culture works, cultural factors are essential but are inadequate to understand the ebb and flow of how effectively communities respond to the problems they face. The first clue from Bowen regarding similarities in family and societal mental processing emerged from the care of criminal delinquents in households. The parents of such communities send the word, "We love you no matter what you do." The parents give in to the kid rather than they hold the line, despite impassioned warnings about honesty and often harsh punishments. The kid protests the parents and is adept at detecting their roles' confusion. To get past the parents, the child feels controlled and lies. Of their punishments, he is insensitive. Parents attempt to monitor the infant, but they are mostly unsuccessful.

Bowen felt that the courts were much like the guardians of delinquents throughout the 1960s. The perpetrator was regarded by those in the youth justice system as a survivor of poor parents. They sought to consider him and in the expectation of effecting an improvement in his behavior, also minimized the implications of his acts. When the suspect is a repeat abuser, the justice system conveyed its dissatisfaction and levied strict sentences, as did the parents. This awareness of a transition in one social institution caused Bowen to find that other organizations, such as schools and legislatures, were undergoing similar shifts. An anxiety-driven regression in functioning is the downward slope in communities struggling with delinquency. In a recession, individuals behave to ease the pressure of the moment rather than act on purpose and a long-term perspective. After World War II, a regressive trend started to unfold in culture. It escalated some during the 1950s and accelerated quickly during the 1960s. The "symptoms of social decline include a rise in crime and aggression, a growing incidence of divorce, an increasingly litigious mentality, increased polarization between race classes, fewer principled leadership decision-making, the epidemic of opioid addiction, an increase in bankruptcy, and an emphasis on privileges over obligations.

Human cultures are undergoing cycles of their past of decline and development. Factors such as the demographic boom, a sense of shrinking boundaries and the loss of natural capital appear to be contributing to the present regression. Bowen expected that like a family in a regression, the present regression would occur until the consequences arising from choosing the easier path out on challenging situations overwhelmed the discomfort involved with behaving on a long-term perspective. He believed that it would take place by the middle of the twenty-first century and that human beings would exist in greater harmony with nature.

Example

In a time of social regression, it is tougher for families to raise children than in a calmer period. It is more challenging for less differentiated parents such as Michael and Martha to retain a line with their children by loosening norms of culture. In certain school systems, grade inflation allows it easy for students to pass classes with fewer effort. In the litigious world, they also face litigation from disgruntled parents as schools decide to hold the line over what they should do with their pupils. The incidence of opioid and alcohol addiction offers parents more items for their teens to think over. An increased child emphasis in the society is defined by the recent cultural decline. There is a great deal of concern concerning the next decade. Parents, both to help them and to track their behavior, are blamed for being too involved with their own pursuits to be properly accessible to their children. The detractors of parenting tend to understand the emotional strength that causes such resentment as kids like Amy complain that they feel disconnected from their parents and separated from their beliefs. The critics proved that the parents were adding some than what they had already done.

The several challenges young people have as evidence for their status are mentioned by individuals who promote greater emphasis on youth. That is exactly what the child-focused parents have been doing all along that the child's issues are using as excuses for increasing the emphasis on them. The growth of the difficulties that young people have is part of an emotional process of culture. For individuals to analyze their own exposure to social decline and to reflect on themselves rather than concentrate on developing the future generation, a more productive direction will be.

Chapter 2

Self-Development

It's a plain truth: when you do, life just gets easier. Act on themselves and they'll pursue the rest. And the good news is that to strengthen yourself, you don't need a massive makeover-a few basic habits will go a long way to improving your sense of well-being and making your days truly meaningful.

With that in mind, here are 15 activities for self-development that can help you become the strongest version of yourself:

1. Plan forward

For the following day, make a to-do list before you head to bed. This way, you can realize precisely what lies ahead and will maximize your time effectively-it will also save you from worrying about everything you have to do for a sleepless night.

2. Get the Transfer

Through releasing mood-boosting endorphins into the brain, not only does exercising enhance your emotional wellbeing, but you can feel positive at doing something better for the body, and your body will thank you in kind. To cause a cascade of those feel-good hormones, even just 20 minutes of aerobic exercise a day is enough.

3. Try New Something

If it's moving to an unfamiliar area of the world or just taking another path to function, going out of your comfort zone helps you more resilient of transition, which can improve the self-confidence in turn.

4. Laugh Out Noisy

Laughing is one of the most therapeutic activities you might do for yourself every day according to study. So, enjoy time with funny buddies or your own TV series. "A day without laughter is a day wasted, as Charlie Chaplin said."

5. Find A Mentor

There's no quicker way to develop yourself than to make others focus on your priorities for you. Many who recruit coaches show generating dramatically more and faster) performance on average than if they had gone it alone.

6. Keep A Report

When you compose, you can get an inside glimpse into your emotions, and be able to see trends in your life that make you happy or unhappy, relaxed, or angry. You will then get to grasp your own motivations and impulses more. In brief, a journal is a realistic place to discover more about yourself, because you will better yourself as you know yourself.

7. Count off Your Blessings

To make you enjoy what you have in existence, maintain a regular appreciation list. Studies suggest that individuals who are willing to maintain appreciation are more happy with their life in general, and are often more physically balanced, and that being grateful for items that are sometimes missed on a regular basis yields countless benefits.

8. Achieve Away

Data often indicates that people with close family or social links are normally happier than those who lack a network of support. Prepare or check out events with friendly family members and acquaintances where you can encounter other people, such as attending a band, class, or support group.

9. Say 'No'

It might only be two small letters, but this is your gentle warning that a full sentence is no." Burnout arises quickly, so investing time refueling and protecting your own well-being is important. Do not go if you don't want to go to a dance. Talk up if you are stressed by your workload. Self-care isn't egotistical.

10. Forward Pay It

By supporting someone, you support yourself, too, honestly. Not only does lending a hand improve emotional health, but it may also lead to a longer existence, evidence reveals. Self-confidence self-esteem and overall well-being are all greatly influenced by volunteering.

11. Stop Saying

Yeah, you need to talk often to blow off steam, but moaning for the sake of complaining is counterproductive and may make you feel frustrated or irritated in the process. Follow things up with a positive approach that can eliminate potential concerns if you find anything to gripe over.

12. Seize the Day

Bear in mind of course, the good lessons learnt from the past, however as Ralph Waldo Emerson said, "Finish every day and be done with it." Today has its own gifts and to be open to them, you need to be 100% present. And then would the visions show themselves tomorrow.

13. Stop to compare

Comparison is the robber of joy," Theodore Roosevelt said the former American president was correct. Since the least we know about ourselves is usually contrasted to the best we expect about others, similarities are unjust. More fundamentally, though,

contrast places the emphasis on the wrong person.
Only one life, yours, will rule you.

14. Prioritizing Yourself

Avoid putting the backburner to your wishes.
Hey, support others, but also help yourself. If there
has ever been a time for you to fulfil your dream and
pursue everything that appeals to you this is the time.

15. Enjoy the ride

Offer positivity control. Love yourself, love
everybody, enjoy this life and appreciate it. It is a gift
to unwrap each day with fresh and eager eyes to look
upon. Have fun above all!

CHAPTER 3
EMOTIONAL INTELLIGENCE IN LOVE AND RELATIONSHIPS

By relational intelligence, control of personal relationships may be strengthened. Data shows that individuals with higher levels of emotional intelligence lead more fulfilling careers than those with low emotional intelligence, and nurture stronger relationships. The capacity to recognize one's own emotions and those of others is known as emotional intelligence. It is the capacity to harness these impulses and to handle them. The key realms of emotional intelligence are central. Each domain's discovery will show why emotional intelligence will help strengthen relationships.

Self-awareness is about managing and growing our capacity to deal with our own feelings. There are numerous questions we pose about ourselves in partnerships. For instance, did I correctly discipline my child? Will I tolerate my wife being career-oriented and spending so much time at work? Does it seem appropriate that my partner spends more time on the golf course than at home? The self-awareness method is quick. It is priceless to become mindful of how you respond to circumstances by accepting how you cope with situations at home. Conversely, it can contribute to distractions, disagreements, and a bad friendship to have little knowledge. A good comprehension and the opportunity to resolve matters will also contribute to stronger partnerships. At the start of each week, one recommendation to improve self-awareness will be to discuss plans. To improve self-awareness self-reflection is often a helpful technique. Reflection helps persons to truly grasp their own thoughts and the impact on the husband/wife of these acts. In turn, greater self-awareness contributes to an enhanced combination between home, job, and social life.

The concept of self-regulation is linked to learning how your body responds to feelings. It is possible to categories feelings as optimistic or bad. Good thoughts provide individuals with comments that contribute to improved direction and concentration. In addition, individuals who have good thoughts would be healthier and feel emotionally healthy. Through thoughts of despair, tension, anxiety and even depression, harmful emotions power the body. Such challenges induce people to lose power. People can also learn to control how they feel and consider the feelings of their spouse. It is crucial to control the feelings as interactions fluctuate between pleasure and depression. It encourages healthier thinking patterns if one can be in control of their thoughts. For e.g., it may be related to fluctuating feelings to help your wife during post-natal trauma, missing a loved one or moving home. By knowing your mind-set, accept your emotions and resolve harmful feelings. Identify how you feel, for instance, by circumstances that cause good and unpleasant feelings. Act with one's loved ones by acknowledging and sharing emotions. By listening to music or taking part in training, staying confident may be done.

Motivation is an inner drive for all human life that is positive. Human existence may be almost non-existent without inspiration. It is beneficial to be inspired and may help foster partnerships. Satisfaction can improve by arranging days off to connect with families. In giving added motivation, partnering for your spouse may be beneficial. An ideal and reliable way of learning what is expected is to provide a weekly approach. Examples of plans might involve training together at the gym, seeing a movie together or visiting the garden center together. While it is appropriate that jobs and fatigue can get in the way of family life, it is often advised that the essence of family ideals should not be dispensed and that doing it together can boost levels of enthusiasm and reinforce and improve relationships.

When helping each other, empathy is important. It may be counterproductive to not be empathetic to your loved one and should be tackled. Empathy is about awareness, desire and understanding of wants. It will be beneficial to define partner expectations and explore how to fulfil them to encourage empathy. We must wonder if we recognize the wishes of our loved ones. Are we worthy of worrying about what they say or do? We should strive not to be so self-centered on me but actually be all rounded up about us.' Exploring ways to help each other stimulates empathic impulses and desires.

Emotional intelligence is in conclusion, a valuable term that can promote stronger partnerships.

How emotional intelligence (EQ) impacts relationships?

Emotional intelligence (EQ) is the secret to enduring interpersonal relationships, primarily because it makes one so mindful of the continually happening shifts between ourselves and others, big and tiny. You'll have the sensitivity that one of us is still searching for in a significant other by constructing your EQ. By active sensitivity and intuition, you'll instinctively feel the little adjustments in the dynamics of your romance that signify a need for intervention.

We have the potential to pursue the kind of love we all dream of, profound affection, shared compassion, true devotion, soulful concern, purely because of empathy, our intrinsic capacity to exchange emotional experience. But we require all the talents of a high EQ to achieve the height of romance: keen emotional sensitivity to prevent mistaking infatuation or desire with enduring love; acceptance of feelings that might damage a relationship if allowed to fester; and a diligent active awareness to understand what works and what is not.

Building emotionally intelligent romantic relationships

We don't have to pick the wrong lovers, wind up in different broken partnerships, or let our long-term partnerships seep out the romance. We don't have to cause competing desires to come between two persons who value each other. In our life of marriage, we don't have to resign ourselves to loneliness or bickering.

We have the potential to achieve the kind of love we all dream of, profound affection and shared compassion, true devoted, soulful care, purely because of sensitivity and our natural capacity to exchange emotional experience. Yet we require all the talents of a high EQ to accomplish certain partnership objectives:

- Astute human consciousness to prevent misunderstood infatuation or desire for enduring love

- Acceptance of feeling feelings that if allowed to fester, might affect a relationship and

- Watchful, active knowledge of what works and what does not.

Fortunately, when you embark upon passion, your EQ may not need to be peaked. Falling in love acts as a motivation for the reeducation of the heart for many citizens. That's why in their eighties, some of the most intensely romantic lovers are: they learn that two high EQs add up to a romance that never stops rising, never loses excitement, and often strengthens both individually and collectively.

Chapter 4
Tips on How to Cope with a Crisis or Trauma

As a by-product, any transition brings tension. Events in our lives are often, however, stressful enough to cause a disaster, and tension levels are often unmanageable. These emergencies involve being afflicted with a severe health problem, coping with the effects of a natural catastrophe, or being directly impacted by a human accident, but a crisis can often be triggered by incidents of lesser magnitude.

Healthy Ways to Cope with a Crisis

There are some safe approaches to work with and get to the other side of a crisis? When grappling with a situation, here are few tips to bear in mind.

Rely on the value of what

It's vital to priorities your energies when coping with the consequences of a disaster. It is an achievement to just get through the day, so paring down the tasks should be necessary to just do that.

Request take-out so that you can cut back on shopping and preparing, set on hold unwanted obligations, and only concentrate on what actually needs to be achieved so that your physical and mental resources can be conserved.

Find Support

If people recognize the pain, odds are they're going to give help; now is the moment to take it up. By assisting with chores or having a friendly ear, let your loved ones lighten your burden. When you are up to it and they require more you will return the favor later.

You will feel happier by getting assistance, because from being willing to do more to improve, people would feel better. That's what is better done by friends.

Reduce Your Stress Response

The stress response of your body can be activated and remain triggered when you encounter a crisis (or even when someone near to you experiences a crisis), holding you in a state of continuous stress.

In the middle or during a disaster, it can be challenging to feel relaxed" but you should practice strategies of stress management that may decrease the severity of your stress levels, help you reverse the stress reaction, and feel more strong in the face of what comes next.

Process Your Feelings

Whether you are writing in your diary, talking to a close friend, or visiting a psychiatrist, to help integrate it is necessary to bring words into your experience.

You may be inclined to suppress your emotions while you go through the problem, for fear that you would 'wallow' too long and become 'stuck', but expressing your feelings helps you to move through them and let them go.

Take Care of Yourself

Make sure to follow a balanced diet, get adequate sleep, workout frequently, and do other stuff to maintain the body working at its highest, to stop contributing to your issues.

Try to do any stuff that you typically love, such as watching a movie, reading a nice novel, or planting, to ease any of the tension you are going through.

Be Patient with Yourself

People who cope with a tragedy or depression often question if their negative responses are an indication of vulnerability or if they're doing it the 'right way. Although there are more and fewer safe approaches to cope with troubling conditions, remain patient with your thoughts and answers to stuff.

After a significant or even mild trauma, feeling 'not yourself' is normal, and embracing yourself and your emotions can make you feel happier and more effectively manage problems.

Seek Help When Needed

Even after many weeks, whether you have unwanted thoughts and emotions, have frequent flashbacks, or are unable to go through your life the way you need to because of your response to the trauma, you might want to chat about your condition

with a therapist to make sure you have the care you
need.

And though you don't have some big issues but
only believe like talking to somebody may be a smart
idea, it's best to err on the side of getting more
support. It's an informed and accountable way to take
care of yourself.

Breathe

Breathing is one of the most important resources
we have. It is natural to hold one's breath while in a
crisis. A warning in the whole body is transmitted by
the fight or flight reaction. Both excessive processes
shut down, muscles contract, and the bloodstream is
pumped with dopamine, which magnifies fear and
frustration. When you hold your breath or breathe in a
shallow manner, the entire body is limited, and the
symptoms of anxiety escalate.

So, take a long, slow breath and release yourself with a sigh. A sigh provides the body a cue to relax. Ask the person to take some long, slow breaths for you. When you have practiced little else, breathing deeply makes us face things because oxygen spreads across our entire system while we breathe deeply. We're going to start calming down and getting calmer. Encourage the person to continue to take long deep, steady breaths, with a sigh releasing them.

Honesty

Recognize what is taking place. Let the entity know that you care. Admit that you feel frightened or confused and don't really know what to do, however you're willing to be with her or him here. "Although the individual has a great emotional experience, for honesty or fact, they are likely to have very sharp radar, otherwise known as a "meter" (technical term J). Stop utilizing denial and platitudes. Typically, people enjoy and comfortable when others are truthful with them. Denial doesn't support anyone. Admitting that you may feel powerless and wish you had a way to make the person feel better is okay.

Control

They are generally hyper-vigilant when someone is in an interpersonal crisis. The situation would normally be worsened by some effort to regulate an individual in crisis. Let yourself realize that you want to help them find out what they want and need, and that you are there for them.

Presence

A solid presence is really calming. Rely about what is occurring right now to remain involved in the case. It pulls you out of this moment to reflect on what has been in the past or could happen in the future which finds it impossible to react to what is occurring now. Do not over-respond. Speak quietly, gently, continue to breathe slowly and profoundly, concentrate on the individual, and have a stable presence.

Suspend the need to fix

It is not helpful now to continue to brainstorm ideas to 'fix' the problem. Instead of really getting support, attempting to solve the problem is often about the helper having to feel in charge. Think of what in moments of depression, has motivated you.

Deep Listening

Listen, listen, listen. Listen, listen. Tell the person that you are involved in what is happening to him or her. And if you don't hear what the entity is doing, listen. Suspend your own judgement to acknowledge that something is significant, even though you don't see what it is. Try to find yourself in a spot of curiosity. In its coping capacity, the psyche's inner workings are very brilliant. The method will also become very interesting as we can step on from attempting to monitor and interrupt the process.

Expressing Emotions

Enable emotions to be communicated by the person. Only bear witness to these sentiments. When you are having difficulty being the emotions of the entity, confess it to yourself and the individual. Because of our trouble being around them, the person may feel guilty for the feelings of others or may be unwilling to convey their own true feelings. Setting limitations is okay. Let the person realize that if they are not disruptive, you can keep room for their emotions. If it's a normal feeling of frustration, consider pounding a cushion, stomping in the woods, creating noises like growling or toning, etc. It is also part of the trigger of an internal distress to mask emotions.

Trust the Process

Be mindful that the first stage in the process of freeing and reorganizing one's existence into a deeper sense of authenticity and wholeness is always an internal crisis. Sometimes, breakdown is a move to breakthrough. Let the person realize that you believe that they are going through a significant transition and that you are eager to help them find what they need.

Ask what is needed

Given what it seems like most individuals, most of the time, realize what they need. Ask the client what they feel they need. Please help them figure out what works for them.

The Basics

It needs an internal tragedy to get back to fundamentals. There really is very little that needs to be achieved. What you need to think on is health, drink, rest, and maybe a stroll. Sugary food can be stopped. A high protein snack helps the soil and balances the thoughts. Make sure the person is consuming plenty of water. A successful grounding strategy is walking or lying on the earth. For some minutes, grasping someone's ankles softly (with permission) brings their vitality back into their body. It is also a very exhausting mental problem. To recover the energy lost, the person can require a great deal of sleep. You need enough rest as well.

Providing Comfort

A person in distress sometimes feels ungrounded and unsupported. They might like a warm bath or cover themselves in a warm blanket. Ask the person if they'd like a hug or encourage you to keep them. Sitting on the floor with your back to a wall or sturdy piece of furniture is a good way of holding others to offer comfort. Make the individual sit in front of you, lean back against you, enabling you to comfort him or her softly with your arms supporting them. He urged them to sigh and breathe deeply. This is a healthy

opportunity to relieve anxiety and they will also

surrender into a deeper position of comfort as they

feel encouraged. If emotional relief often comes with

this surrender, do not be shocked. You may offer to

massage the back or feet of an individual, too. If this

were you, think of what would make you feel more

comfortable and thought about.

Spiritual Support

For both you and the person, follow whatever

spiritual support and faith makes sense. Ask for this

condition to be transformed. You don't need to see

what it would feel like. Be accessible to the idea that

there is a greater artistic intellect that runs all the time

across all things. Each moment has the power to

change.

CONCLUSION

T his write-up acts as a book review; I hear the remarkably easy talent behind you. When they read side by side, it can act as a reference for readers who seek a proper description of the book or others who require an interpretation. For better interpretation without inserting or withdrawing from the main message of the novel, this overview is a comprehensive chapter by chapter overview of all the important points outlined and condensed. This quick summary can help the reader quickly capture the intent of the novel, whether the reader wants to read the book or not.